Traction Engines

PETER WALLER

NOSTALGIA ROAD

First published by Crécy Publishing Limited
2016

© Text: UPSL 2015
© Photographs: As credited;
historic images on pages 5, 21, 24, 32, 35, 39,
41, 45, 46, 52, 54, 57, 60 are reproduced from
Grace's Guide to British Industrial History

A CIP record for this book is available from
the British Library

ISBN 9781908347374

Printed in Malta by Melita Press

Nostalgia Road is an imprint of
Crécy Publishing Limited
1a Ringway Trading Estate
Shadowmoss Road
Manchester M22 5LH

www.crecy.co.uk

Front Cover: Recorded at Knebworth on 2 September
1978, this showman's engine DP 4418 was manufactured
by Fowler (14425/1916). At the time of writing the engine
carries the name Carry On. *J M Jarvis/Online Transport
Archive*

Rear Cover Top: North Thames Gas Board No 267
(CGW 845) was a Sentinel (9227) and is seen on
Westminster Bridge Road on 9 November 1950.
John Meredith/Online Transport Archive (156/1)

Rear Cover Bottom: Recorded during the early summer
of 1966 en route to Southampton, NO 4630 Wilbur is a
Fowler-built Class BB ploughing engine (14712/1917).
With an impressive nhp of 14, the engine weighs 16 tons.
Alan S Clayton/ Online Transport Archive (AC15-28)

Contents Page: Seen at the tramway museum at
Crich in 1974, VM 4536 is a Foden steam wagon
(13120/1928) that at the time of writing carries the
name *Midnight Rambler. Alan S Clayton/Online
Transport Archive (102-74-38)*

CONTENTS

Introduction

That steam represented a potential means of transportation was recognised from the mid-18th century. Nicolas-Joseph Cugnot's 'Fardier à vapeur' of 1769, for example, was a 'fire engine for transporting wagons and especially artillery' designed for use by the French military. In 1801 Richard Trevithick built *Puffing Devil*; this was a steam-driven vehicle that possessed one vertical cylinder. The cylinder, with its piston, acted directly to the wheels via connecting rods and the vehicle was capable of about 9mph on the level. This pioneering vehicle, however, self-destructed on its first run. Two years later Trevithick followed *Puffing Devil* up with the *London Steam Carriage*. Initially, when operating in London, this was successful but the venture failed to find sufficient financial support and did not last.

Trevithick's most important contribution, however, was the development of the use of high-pressure steam. From his pioneering work, there were a number of advances during the first half of the 19th century. In the 1830s the roads of Britain played host to steam carriages operated, inter alia, by Walter Hancock, Sir Goldsworthy Gurney and John Scott Russell. These were, however, to be relatively unsuccessful for two reasons: firstly, they were heavy and the condition of the roads at the time was not good; and, secondly, the use of the roads controlled by the Turnpike Trusts meant that the vehicles were subject to high tolls.

In Britain, a further factor behind the relatively slow adoption of steam technology for road transport was the legislative framework that covered such vehicles. In 1861 the Locomotive Act was passed; this resulted in speed limits of 5mph in towns and 10mph in the countryside. This was followed by the 1865 Locomotives on Highways Act; this reduced further the maximum speed limit to 2mph and 4mph in towns and countryside respectively. It was this act that also imposed the requirement that a man with a red flag had to walk in front of every self-propelled vehicle. The act also permitted individual local authorities to regulate the hours that such vehicles could be used and stipulated that all mechanically powered road vehicles must have three drivers.

Although the use of steam-propelled vehicles on the nation's roads was effectively thwarted by legislation, there were other areas where the development of self-propelled steam vehicles could progress. This was most notably the case in

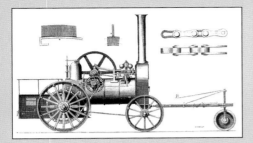

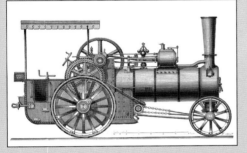

Left: The company of Marshall, Sons & Co starting the manufacture of traction engines in 1876; this example was produced the following year.

Above: Produced the same year (1877) was this 8nhp agricultural engine manufactured by Wallis & Steevens of Basingstoke.

Top left: An early Aveling & Porter self-propelled agricultural engine. This was produced in 1861, two years after the company had pioneered the development of the traction engine by converting a horse-drawn portable engine.

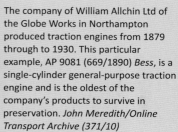

The company of William Allchin Ltd of the Globe Works in Northampton produced traction engines from 1879 through to 1930. This particular example, AP 9081 (669/1890) *Bess*, is a single-cylinder general-purpose traction engine and is the oldest of the company's products to survive in preservation. *John Meredith/Online Transport Archive (371/10)*

Owned when photographed at the West Sussex Traction Engine Rally, North Heath, Pulborough on 12 August 1956 by M Lugg, BP 5919 *Achilles* is a Burrell (3201/1910) single crank compound general-purpose traction engine. It weighs 11 tons. *John Meredith/Online Transport Archive (371/8)*

agriculture. John Fowler was to demonstrate the use of steam power in the draining and ploughing of fields from 1850 onwards, but it was not until 1859 that the principle of the self-propelled steam engine was established when the Kent-based firm of Aveling & Porter converted a portable engine that had been built earlier by Clayton & Shuttleworth.

The second half of the 19th century was to see further developments in the efficacy of the self-propelled steam engine. The poor quality of the roads and the impact of the Locomotive Acts meant that, for much of the late 19th century, traction engines were relatively small and slow. In was not until 1896 that the 1865 act was superseded by a new Locomotives on Highways Act. The new legislation removed the requirement for the man with the red flag, increased speed limits (to 5mph for vehicles weighing more than two tons) and created a new category of vehicle — the

Pictured en route to Southampton in the early summer of 1966 is HO 5815 *Boxer's Beauty*, a Wallis & Steevens (7115/1910) single-cylinder general-purpose engine. *Alan S Clayton/Online Transport Archive (AC15-32)*

light locomotive of under three tons in weight — that did not require the three drivers. It was this act that paved the way for the development of the private motorcar.

With the relaxed restrictions, there was a considerable impetus towards the construction of larger and more powerful traction engines. In many respects, the golden age of the traction engine was a relatively short period, from the passing of the 1896 act through to World War 1. It was the war that was to have a dramatic impact on the nature of road transport. Although, inevitably, the war provided a stimulus to production — a large number of ploughing engines were built by John Fowler & Co, for example, as the area of cultivation in the country expanded to meet wartime needs — it also saw the rapid development of the internal-combustion engine. Moreover, with the cessation of hostilities in 1918, a vast number of military surplus vehicles flooded onto the market; these vehicles were to revolutionise both the road haulage and coaching industries during the 1920s.

Despite the savings that the operation of a petrol-driven lorry could operate, the manufacturers of steam-powered vehicles continued to invest in new products during the 1920s and 1930s but the tide was turning against them. During the period, the operators of steam vehicles found that there were tighter restrictions on emissions and speed, all of which aided the competitive advantage that petrol- and diesel-powered vehicles had. In 1933, following the Salter report into road

Manufactured by Charles Burrell & Sons TD 4276 (3618/1914) is a tractor traction engine pictured at the Lambton Park Traction Engine Rally on 15 June 1958. At the time the engine was called *Princess Royal*; at the time of writing, carrying the name *The Scout*, TD 4276 is now bereft of its overall canopy. *Tony Wickens/Online Transport Archive (2022)*

funding, a tax based upon vehicle axle weight was introduced. This was an inevitable disadvantage to steam-powered vehicles as they were generally much heavier than those powered by the internal-combustion engine.

In theory, however, steam-powered vehicles had one great advantage over the internal-combustion engine in that they relied upon domestically produced coal — some 950,000 tons annually at the peak of the industry — rather than imported oil. However, even this advantage was undermined in 1934 when the then Minister of Transport, Oliver Stanley, reduced the duty on fuel oils whilst simultaneously increasing to £100 per annum the Road Fund duty on road locomotives.

The interwar period saw a steady, but inexorable, decline in the numbers of manufacturers as companies moved into the production of petrol- or diesel-engined vehicles or failed completely. One of the great names — Charles Burrell & Sons Ltd — sold out in 1928 and its factory at Thetford was to close the following year. Leyland ceased to produce steam-powered vehicles in 1926 and William Achin Ltd stopped the following year. Foden, despite a split between the pro- and anti-diesel factions that resulted in the creation of ERF, itself ceased to build steam wagons in 1934. Another of the great names — Richard Garrett & Sons — which had taken over Burrell and produced the last Burrell-badged vehicles at Leiston, manufactured its

Owned at the time by H H Naylor, this compound general-purpose traction engine, AP 9281 was seen at the Andover Rally on 12 May 1956. It was built by the Andover-based company W Tasker & Sons Ltd (1776/1918); this company manufactured its first traction engines in 1869. The company had a somewhat chequered career financially, going into liquidation in both 1903 and 1926; reconstructed in 1932 as Taskers of Andover, production thereafter was concentrated upon the manufacture of trailers with traction engine production ceasing in the late 1920s. *John Meredith/Online Transport Archive (367/4)*

The Preston-based manufacturer Atkinson Lorries Ltd was a relatively late entrant into the field of steam wagon production, not building its first example until 1916. Capitalising on the post-war boom in production, the company built 545 by the time manufacture ceased in 1929. This example, CK 209 (72/1918) *Her Majesty*, was an undertype tipping wagon and is pictured at Lightwater Valley on 12 September 1981 when owned by T Varley. *John Meredith/Online Transport Archive (978/3)*

Lincoln-based Clayton & Shuttleworth produced self-propelled steam engines between 1860 and 1929, when the company went into liquidation; this example, BH 7651 (48224/1919) *Valiant* is a general-purpose engine and is seen at the Saffron Walden Steam Festival on 15 June 1957. *John Meredith/Online Transport Archive (381/2)*

last vehicles in 1939. A handful of manufacturers survived into the post-World War 2 era but even these were short-lived; Aveling-Barford, for example, ceasing to produce steamrollers in 1950 and Sentinel produced its final steam lorries two years later.

Whilst steam-powered vehicles continued to be seen on Britain's in the post-war years, they were in steep decline. The last commercial use of a showman's engine occurred in 1958 although steamrollers were still a regular sight through the 1960s; indeed, some of the latter were to be used in the construction of the early motorways — old technology being used to create the modern age.

This was not to be the end of the story as preservation saw a large number of these popular vehicles survive. From the early 1950s onwards, regular events were held nationwide to enable those interested in traction engines to see and show them. These events — such as the Great Dorset Steam Fair held annually each

When recorded at Callington in the 1960s, this Garrett BJ 5597 (33987/1920) was in the livery of J H Dingle, a contractor of Kelly Bray. The engine is still extant but now in a very different form, having been converted into a showman's engine with extended canopy and named *The Leader*. *J M Jarvis/Online Transport Archive*

NT 7184 is a William Foster & Co Ltd (14568/1925) single-cylinder general-purpose engine that, at the time of writing carried the name *Matilda*. By 1925 production of traction engines was in steep decline as economics increasingly favoured the internal-combustion engine. *J M Jarvis/Online Transport Archive*

Steamrollers

For many the steamroller was perhaps the most visible for of steam-powered road transport, particularly in the years after the end of World War 2. This was partly the result of the fact that steamrollers continued in use through to the 1960s and early 1970s; indeed construction of the early stages of the future M1 in the late 1950s and early 1960s saw the use of steamrollers.

The earliest steamrollers were demonstrated in 1860 by Louis Lemoine in France and in Britain during 1863 by William Clark, who was Chief Municipal Engineer of Calcutta in India, and his partner William Batho, of Birmingham. It was the Kent-based manufacturer Aveling & Porter that was the first builder to sell steamrollers commercially, producing a prototype model based around a 12hp traction engine in 1866 which was followed the next year by a more practical machine. The 1867 roller weighed some 30 tons and was tested in Chatham, Rochester and London, proving to be a great success. With production in hand, Aveling & Porter steamrollers were sold around Britain and overseas. The steamroller offered a considerable improvement in efficiency over the earlier, horse-drawn road rollers. A New York-based engineer commented that 'in one day's rolling at a cost of 10 dollars, as much work was accomplished as in two days' rolling with a 7 ton roller drawn by eight horses at a cost of 20 dollars a day.' Aveling & Porter were to dominate the production of steamrollers, regularly improving the design of the vehicles. For example, at the 1881 Royal Agricultural Show the company displayed a model with fully steerable front rollers.

To all intents and purposes, the steamroller was a conventional traction engine but, instead of wheel, was fitted with rollers. These normally comprised two large wheels at the rear combined with a single wide roller at the front. The latter was, however, often split into two narrow drums as this made steering the roller much easier. There were variants, however; one company, Robey & Co, favoured the production of tandem machines, which had two wide rollers — one at the front and one at the back. There were also convertible machines, that could be operated as either traction engines or as steamrollers through replacing the wheels with rollers. These vehicles offered considerable flexibility to customers since they could be used for haulage during the winter months and for road rolling during the better weather. Other features of the steamroller included a scraper bar, that could be used to keep the front rollers clean of muck and this ensure a smoother road surface, and a scarifier on the rear. This was designed to be used to remove the original road surface before the new surface was laid.

A derelict Aveling & Porter (2204/1886) steam roller, NR 239, stands on a bomb site at Effra Road, Brixton on 18 June 1950. This was delivered new to the Idle Local Board in Yorkshire. Owned by Alfred J Ward of Egham from 1930, the roller was sold for scrap shortly after this photograph was taken. *John Meredith/Online Transport Archive (123/5)*

John Allen & Sons (Oxford) Ltd No 163 EE 5356 was a Fowler single roller (7943/1899) and is seen on the Oxford bypass on 4 September 1955. *John Meredith/Online Transport Archive (361/2)*

This roller (Aveling & Porter DA 5562), which was delivered new to Wolverhampton Corporation, was far away from its original territory when photographed near Brecon on Bwlch Road on 4 September 1955. *John Meredith/Online Transport Archive (360/12)*

An undated photograph taken in the early 1960s records an Aveling & Porter Class C roller (10677/1923). This was a single-cylinder 4nhp machine with a weight of eight tons. *J M Jarvis/Online Transport Archive*

Rowley Plan Hire Co Ltd Marshall-built roller OPC 765 (78724/1925) is pictured under repair at Beddington Lane Depot on 2 December 1950. An Aveling & Porter roller (4855) is visible in the background. *John Meredith/Online Transport Archive (158/8)*

Owned by J O Lugg & Son this Aveling & Porter PO 616 (12427/1929) single roller was recorded at Billingshurst on 6 August 1956. *John Meredith/Online Transport Archive (371/5)*

City of Norwich No 7 — Aveling & Porter VG 2269 (14008/1929)— is a compound roller and is recorded at Carrow Road, Norwich, on 28 June 1956. *John Meredith/Online Transport Archive (369/10)*

Pictured at Witney in 1954, Fowler WU 2071 (16485/1925) *The Iron Lady* is a Class DN1 single-cylinder steamroller. *J M Jarvis/Online Transport Archive*

H Richards & Co Ltd, of Newport in Monmouthshire, No 62 (WD 7354) was an Aveling & Porter compound roller (14100) and is pictured near Abergavenny on 27 August 1955. *John Meredith/Online Transport Archive (356/10)*

The manufacture of steamrollers in Britain continued through to the early 1950s and a significant number have survived into preservation. Steamrollers have also made their mark in films, perhaps most notably in the classic Ealing Comedy *The Titfield Thunderbolt*, released in March 1953. Although ostensibly about the attempted preservation of a closed rural branch line, a steamroller — CH 3282 (a Aveling & Porter Class R10 single-cylinder steamroller [5590/1910]) — driven by Sid James was used by the opponents of the railway to try and thwart the railway's supporters.

Ploughing Engines and Farm Equipment

The ploughing engine represented a distinct type of traction engine. As built, a traction engine was not a practical alternative to the earlier forms of animal- or man-powered plough as it was simply too heavy to work the fields. The movement of the vehicle over the soil would have lead to serious compaction and thus would have made ploughing more difficult.

As a result, ploughing engines were fitted with a large diameter drum driven by separate gearing from the steam engine. A length of wire rope was then wound onto the drum; this rope could then be attached to a plough or other farm implement which could be hauled over the ground whilst the ploughing engine itself remained stationary. The usual working procedure was to use two ploughing engines — one at either end of the field — with the plough hauled between the two. Communication between the two drivers was via the engines' whistles.

The development of the ploughing engine as a practical piece of equipment is generally regarded as being the work of John Fowler (1826-1864). In 1849, following a visit to Ireland shortly after the potato famine, Fowler became convinced that more land could be brought into cultivation if drainage could be improved. As a result he started to look at more efficient methods of land drainage. Drainage was normally achieved through the use of a 'mole' plough to dig a subterranean drainage channel; however, this required considerable power to drag it through the soil and the maximum plough size was reliant upon the power of the horses used.

Fowler's initial work was to find a more efficient form of horse-powered mole. His first development was to take a horse team and use it to power a capstan onto which a rope was fitted that dragged the ploughing engine with its mole plus drainage pipes through the ground. Although not as yet perfected, Fowler was able to display this at the Royal Agricultural Society of England show at Exeter in 1850. He received a silver medal for the device.

The following year Fowler demonstrated a much-improved version at the Great Exhibition. This development saw the ploughing engine remaining stationary at the corner of the field being worked on and so the workload of the horses was expended simply in the movement of the plough across the field via a system of pulleys and a vertical winch. This improved version was demonstrated at the Royal Agricultural Society of England's show at Gloucester in 1853, where it again received a silver medal.

Aveling & Porter BW 4990 (5150/1903) *Prince*, owned when seen at the Saffron Walden Steam Festival on 15 June 1957 by J W Clarke, is a single cylinder 6nhp agricultural engine weighing 8 tons. *John Meredith/Online Transport Archive (381/8)*

Ruston & Hornsby CE 7977 (113043/1920) is a single 6nhp agricultural engine weighing 10 tons. It too is seen at the Saffron Walden Steam Festival on 15 June 1957 when it was owned by C R Pumfrey. *John Meredith/Online Transport Archive (382/1)*

By this date, however, Fowler, who had had earlier experience of working with steam engines, had started to apply the principle of steam power to the problem. In his first attempt to use steam, he reverted to the concept of the original horse-drawn plough of 1850 in which the engine dragged itself and the mole across the field. The inherent problem of the weight of the steam engine meant that this experiment was a failure although, in October 1852, Fowler took out a patent based on this work for 'Improvements in Machinery for draining land'.

With his first steam plough not proving a success, Fowler opted to replicate the style of his second horse-powered plough by placing a stationary engine in the corner of the field to be ploughed. Using winches and a rope, the engine was able to propel the mole successfully to produce the drainage channels. The new version of the steam plough was demonstrated at a meeting held in 1854 at Lincoln by the Royal Agricultural Society of England.

Burrell CL 4483 (3847/1920) is pictured at the Woburn Park Traction Engine Rally on 5 August 1957 coupled to a threshing machine. At the time it was owned by J Bennie, Hanmington, Northamptonshire.
John Meredith/Online Transport Archive (384/12)

The use of a steam engine to improve drainage was thus established; more difficult was to see steam adopted for the actual ploughing of a field. The equipment used for ploughing was much lighter than that used in producing field drains and was thus still well suited for a team of horses. The most significant delay in horse-powered ploughing came with the necessity of turning the team at the end of each run; if Fowler could come up with a plough that did not require turning he was make a steam plough more attractive.

A photograph, taken during 1918, of a Wallis & Steevens-built ploughing engine at work. *The Engineer*

Owned at the time by S Hills, Fowler KE 2728 (13422/1912) *Sunshine* was a 12nhp Class KKS compound superheated ploughing engine and was on display at the Woburn Park Traction Engine Rally on 5 August 1957. *John Meredith/Online Transport Archive (383/7)*

This Fowler ploughing engine AB 9987 (13910/1914) shows to good effect the underslung winding drum. This was the most common arrangement for the drum to be attached to the boiler. *Tony Wickens/Online Transport Archive (2020)*

Fowler designed a frame for a plough with blades at both ends. Through the use of pulleys and a stationary engine more rapid ploughing could be achieved. The first of these ploughs was built by the Ipswich-based company Ransomes & Sims and demonstrated on 10 April 1856. Whilst effective in ploughing — it achieved the ploughing of a one-acre field in an hour — the process of shifting the pulleys after each run caused delays. Fowler further modified the design, using weighted carts with pulleys, and this revised version was shown to the Royal Agricultural Society of England at Chelmsford later in 1856 and at Salisbury the following year.

In 1856 Fowler also patented a method of ploughing using two stationary engines, although as this was much more expensive, he continued to refine further the single-engine version as it was more economic for farmers. The double-engine method, first shown by Fowler at a Royal Agricultural Society of England meeting at Worcester in 1863, was to become the dominant means of ploughing when employed by contractors.

Recorded during the early summer of 1966 en route to Southampton, NO 4630 *Wilbur* is a Fowler-built Class BB ploughing engine (14712/1917). With an impressive nhp of 14, the engine weighs 16 tons. *Alan S Clayton/ Online Transport Archive (AC15-28)*

In all, between 1850 and 1864, when he died, Fowler had taken out, either individually or with partners, some 32 patents on ploughing machines and other agricultural equipment. Manufacture was centred on Leeds and, in 1862, Fowler entered into business, the company eventually becoming John Fowler & Co, one of the country's leading manufacturers of steam engines.

In terms of operation, the winding drum on a ploughing engine could be found in three different positions: horizontally (beneath the boiler); vertically (on one or other side of the boiler); or, concentrically (where the drum encircled the boiler). The most common form, however, was the horizontal (or underslung) version. This form required a longer than usual boiler as extra space was required between the front and rear wheels of the engine. As a consequence, underslung ploughing engines were amongst the longest and largest traction engines to be constructed.

The use of steam on farms rapidly diminished after World War 1 as cheap tractors, powered by the internal combustion engine, came to dominate. Companies like David Brown of Huddersfield manufactured vehicles that were much more flexible and lighter, thus able to work more efficiently across the fields.

Steam Wagons

In an era before the use of the internal combustion engine became widespread, the steam wagon represented a popular form of transport for commercial haulage of freight. There were, in design terms, two basic models — the overtype and the undertype — the difference being in the relative position of the engine to the vehicle's boiler. The majority of early vehicles were fitted with solid tyres, but as pneumatic tyre technology improved, later vehicles generally had pneumatic tyres and older vehicles were converted to use them.

Undertype designs had the engine underneath the chassis whilst the boiler, usually of a vertical type, remained in the cab. The resulting vehicle looked much more like a conventional lorry and had the benefit of offering a more enclosed cab and a shorter length for a given carrying capacity.

The overtype in contrast looked much more like a cross between a traction engine and a lorry. The front end had a cab constructed around a horizontal boiler with a chimney and round smokebox. Behind the engine came a load-carrying platform constructed on a chassis.

The imperative to construct steam wagons came in the late 19th century when restrictions on the use of road vehicles were gradually reduced. Prior to the development of the steam wagon, freight had been carried in wagons that were generally horse-pulled although traction engines could be used as well. Gradually restrictions on the weight limits that could be moved were also increased, which made the use of steam — and later petrol/diesel — power more attractive.

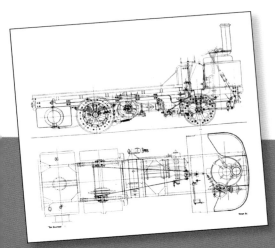

Drawing published in *The Engineer* in 1906 showing the plan and elevation of the pioneering Sentinel Steam Wagon; at this date the company was still based in Glasgow. It would not be until 1915 that a factory was established in Shrewsbury. *The Engineer*

Owned at the time by William Selby, this Sentinel Super CA 6395 (5104/1924) is pictured at the Andover Rally, held at Finkley Manor Farm on 12 May 1956. *John Meredith/Online Transport Archive (367/2)*

In 1901 the War Department held vehicle trials at Aldershot to test the products of a number of manufacturers; a Thornycroft product, an undertype with a chain drive, came out on top although many considered that Foden's entry, a chain-driven overtype, performed better.

During the years leading up to World War 1 there were a number of improvements to the design of the steam wagon as the leading manufacturers — such as Wallis & Steevens, Sentinel and Foden — sought to gain a competitive advantage. Sentinel's improvements to the undertype were perhaps the most significant and many of the other manufacturers, such as Fowler and Foden, sought to produce competitors, with varying degrees of success.

The golden age of the steam wagon was probably in the years immediately after World War 1 with Sentinel's C-type of 1922 and Super Sentinel of 1923 being pivotal. In 1926 Garrett produced the first three-axle steam wagon; this was an attempt to try and increase the load capacity of the steam wagon. Early attempts to increase the weight carried had resulted in the development of tractors with articulated trailers; braking problems, however, meant that these were prone to jack-knife.

North Thames Gas Board No 267 (CGW 845) was a Sentinel (9227) and is seen on Westminster Bridge Road on 9 November 1950. *John Meredith/Online Transport Archive (156/1)*

By this date owned by T T Broughton & Sons Ltd but originally new to new to Fuller, Smith & Turner and used until 1948, this Foden overtype wagon AN 9568 (13138/1929) was present at the Woburn Park Traction Engine Rally on 5 August 1957. *John Meredith/Online Transport Archive (384/2)*

During the mid- to late 1920s the road haulage industry gradually shifted away from the steam wagon. Improvements to the internal combustion engine, alongside the significant number of ex-military vehicles rendered surplus at the end of World War 1, made the steam wagon less competitive. They were costly to manufacture and more expensive to operate. It was estimated that the saving from using a three-ton petrol truck over a steam wagon of the same capacity was £100 per month.

Earlier in the story, steam wagons had benefited from legislative changes; during the late 1920s and early 1930s the reverse applied. Amongst impositions were the 'wetted tax', where tax was paid according to the wetted area of the boiler, and the axle weight tax, which was introduced in 1933. The latter was the result of the Salter report on road funding; this argued that the cost of road repairs should be based upon the axle weight of the vehicles so as to avoid the charge that the road freight industry was gaining a competitive edge over the railways by not paying for maintenance. Given that the axle weight of a steam wagon was much higher than that of the equivalent lorry powered by an internal combustion engine, the steam wagon was again at a competitive disadvantage.

Whilst the steam wagon used home produced coal and the internal combustion engine relied on imported oil, a further change, in 1934 when the then Minister of Transport Oliver Stanley, reduced the duty on imported oil whilst raising the Road Fund duty on steam wagons and other road locomotives, again undermined the steam wagon industry.

The consequence of these policies was that most manufacturers of steam wagons ceased their construction — Leyland, for example, produced its last steam wagon in 1926 — with only a handful of the 160 or so original manufacturers trying to survive against the prevailing market conditions. Whilst many steam wagons were scrapped during the late 1930s as the economics of the road haulage industry saw a massive shift towards the petrol- or diesel-powered lorry, a number were still operational during and after World War 2.

Owned by A Fearnley, Castleford, Yorks when recorded at the Woburn Park Traction Engine Rally on 5 August 1957, Sentinel SE 4013 (9086/1934) was an S4 wagon built in the year that the company launched the S4 model. *John Meredith/Online Transport Archive (384/10)*

Travelling Showmen

From the late 19th century onwards, travelling showmen and circuses made great use of traction engines for the movement of their rides and for powering the various attractions when the showmen had reached their destination.

Whilst based around the normal traction engine, there were features that emphasised that these vehicles were 'special'. In particular, the showman's engines tended to be much more brightly painted and decorated, often incorporating polished brass ornamentation. In addition showman's engines tended to have a full length canopy and be fitted with an extension chimney; the latter was normally carried on brackets on the roof when the vehicle was in transit but would be added to the normal chimney when in use at the showground as a means of ensuring that the smoke and smut did not affect the customers. In order to provide power for the various rides, the engines were generally fitted with a dynamo; these were usually belt-driven from the engine's flywheel.

Apart from the large showman's engines, there were also a number of smaller vehicles used. The showman's tractor was a smaller version of the usual showman's engine; these were often built with a weight of between five and seven tons. The major manufacturer was primarily Richard Garrett & Sons of Leiston, which produced a version based on its successful 4CD tractor, with other builders being Burrell and William Foster.

The ultimate development of the showman's engine were the scenic engines that were first produced in 1920. These engines, designed to work with the heavier fairground rides then being developed, were fitted with a second dynamo — known as the exciter — located behind the chimney. Apart from one experimental model built by John Fowler & Co, the vast majority were built by Charles Burrell & Sons of Thetford, with the first being completed in 1920.

Alongside the purpose-built vehicles, showmen were also adept in acquiring other types of vehicle for use. Whilst a small number of the steam wagons were

Opposite top: Built by Foden (2104/1910), WR 6985 *Prospector* is seen in Southport in 1975 in the livery of Frank Lythgoe of Warburton. This view shows to good effect the chimney extension, carried on the roof, and the dynamo, fitted over the smokebox to generate power for the various rides, that were characteristic of these showmen's engines. *John G Parkinson/Online Transport Archive*

Bottom: When recorded at the Witney Rally in 1954, this showman's engine — Burrell PB 9624 (3489/1913) *King George VI* — was owned by S J Wharton. *J M Jarvis/Online Transport Archive*

Owned by H D Knight, this Foster PP 5649 (14066/1915) is a 4nhp compound showman's tractor and was seen at the Woburn Park Traction Engine Rally on 5 August 1957. *John Meredith/Online Transport Archive (384/11)*

built specifically for showmen — such as Charles Burrell & Sons' No 3883 *Electra*, which was supplied to Charles Summers of Norwich in 1921 — many more were converted from conventional road locomotives.

The use of the traditional showman's engine declined during the 1950s and had ceased entirely by the end of the decade. The popularity of the type saw many of them escape the scrapyard and enter preservation.

Bearng the name of its original manufacturers, this Class B2 compound showman's tractor, HO 2930 (1822/1920) *Little Jim II*, is pictured at Knebworth on 2 September 1978. *J M Jarvis/Online Transport Archive*

Originally owned by Mrs Oadley of Alfreton, Derbyshire, this Fowler FX 6661 (15657/1920) *Kitchener*, a compound showman's road locomotive, was owned by J Crawley when photographed at the Woburn Park Traction Engine Rally on 5 August 1957. *John Meredith/Online Transport Archive (383/4)*

Right: Recorded in 1974, XF 8162 is a Burrell showman's road locomotive (3886/1921). Named *Lord Lascelles* the 8nhp engine weighs 22 tons. *Alan S Clayton/Online Transport Archive (102-74-25)*

Below: Belong to T Sage at the time, this Fowler DH 2545 (14424/1919) *Goliath* is a compound showman's road locomotive and is again seen at the Woburn Park Traction Engine Rally on 5 August 1957. *John Meredith/Online Transport Archive (383/3)*

The Classic Manufacturers

Aveling & Porter

Once the largest manufacturers of steamrollers in the world, Aveling & Porter was based at Rochester in Kent. The business commenced in 1862 through a partnership between Thomas Aveling and Richard Porter. In May that year Aveling & Porter displayed a traction engine at the Bath & West Society show. The engine had been driven the 190 miles over 48 hours prior to the show's opening. The following month, at the International Show of the Agricultural Society, they displayed an agricultural locomotive for ploughing, threshing and general traction purposes.

In 1863 Aveling was awarded a patent for improvements in the construction of traction engines. The following year the company produced its first railway locomotive; it continued in this business until 1926. In 1865 a steamroller was demonstrated in London and, closer to home, in Rochester and Chatham. By 1871, the company employed 300 men and boys.

During the second half of the 19th century the company continued to grow and, by 1895, a total of 1,000 were employed and the company became incorporated as a limited liability company the same year. By the end of the century Aveling & Porter was producing one large road engine per day and, in the decade before World War 1, the company was producing some 70% of the road rollers for the British market.

After World War 1, during which the company produced munitions alongside its steamrollers (but which had resulted in the manufacture of petrol-driven vehicles ceasing), Aveling & Porter were amongst

An 1880 advert for an Aveling & Porter steamroller.

Rowley Plan Hire Co Ltd No 5, an Aveling & Porter roller ME 3266 (4855) is seen at Beddington Lane Depot on 2 December 1950. This roller was registered No 64 with Middlesex County Council. In the background is Marshall OPC 765. *John Meredith/Online Transport Archive (158/9)*

Another Rowley Plan Hire Co Ltd roller, Aveling Barford OPA 684, is also seen at the Beddington Lane Depot on 2 December 1950. *John Meredith/Online Transport Archive (158/7)*

the promoters of the creation of the Agricultural & General Engineers combine in 1919; the purposes of this business, which ultimately acquired control over more than a dozen businesses, was to rationalise the number of manufacturers and, to that effect production of Aveling & Barford steam wagons was transferred to Richard Garrett & Sons.

Agricultural & General Engineers struggled during the late 1920s and, in 1932, finally collapsed with Aveling & Porter emerging from the combine having acquired the assets of Barford & Perkins. In 1934 the company became Aveling-Barford; the new business was part-funded by Ruston & Hornsby of Lincoln with the result that production was transferred from Rochester to Grantham. Going public in 1937, the business continued to build motor and steamrollers until after World War 2 and expanded to other construction equipment. Steamroller manufacture ceased in about 1950.

In all, the company manufactured some 12,200 steam-powered vehicles.

Charles Burrell & Sons

Based at the St Nicholas Works in Thetford in Norfolk and with a history stretching back to 1770, Charles Burrell & Sons was originally a business dealing with agricultural equipment, and produced its first steam engine in 1846. Initially the production was of small portable engines but this soon expanded into self-propelled agricultural vehicles and road vehicles.

Above: A Burrell traction engine of 1862 showing the concept of the Boydell endless railway. The principle was that, by spreading the weight of the locomotive over a greater distance, the engine could be used more widely. Production of equipment using the Boydell system ceased the year that this engine was built.

A Burrell ploughing engine fitted with a vertical winding drum as shown at the Carlisle Royal Agricultural Society of England show of 1880.

CF 3354, seen here at Knebworth on 2 September 1978, is single-crank compound general-purpose traction engine built by Burrell (1902/3505). *J M Jarvis/Online Transport Archive*

By 1851 and the Great Exhibition, the company was employing 59 men and boys. During the 1850s the company concentrated on the development of self-moving steam engines, working closely with James Boydell, who had patented an 'endless railway' device. This was a series of flat feet attached to the outside of the road vehicle's wheels that had the effect of spreading the load more efficiently and thus allowing operation of self-propelled steam vehicles on the poor roads of the mid-19th century. In 1855 the company was licensed to produce vehicles using the Boydell patent and a number of vehicles were built between then and 1862.

However, the Boydell technology proved unsatisfactory and the company then concentrated upon the development of traction engines and road locomotives with more conventional wheels. The company produced its first road locomotives in the late 1870s, with 14 being constructed between 1878 and 1890. The company was formally incorporated as Charles Burrell & Sons Ltd in 1884. In 1889, the company built engine No 1451 *Monarch*; this was one of the first to be built specifically as a showman's engine. The manufacturer of the ornate engines used by showmen was a market that Charles Burrell & Sons was to dominate, largely through its very popular 8nhp single-crank compound design.

When recorded in Southport in 1975, this 10-ton 7nhp Burrell roller TB 3778 (2642/1904) *Ethel* was in the colours of John F Webster of Tarleton. *John G Parkinson/Online Transport Archive*

The company produced its first road roller in 1891 and its first steam lorry a decade later. In 1905, following changed legislation, Charles Burrell & Sons Ltd produced its first road tractor. The production of portable engines ceased in 1908 with some 670 having been constructed. The company's most successful year was 1913; a total of 104 engines were completed with the business concentrating on the production of traction engines for agricultural use and those supplied for travelling showmen.

J P Bury's Burrell showman's road loco NM 257 (2668/1904) *Britannia* is seen at the National Traction Engine Rally held at Appleford on 6 June 1953. *John Meredith/Online Transport Archive (158/7)*

Owned at this date by S J Wharton, this Burrell road loco TA 1973 (3202/1910) is also seen at the National Traction Engine Rally held at Appleford on 6 June 1953. *John Meredith/Online Transport Archive (303/12)*

Farm Engines (Ashington) Ltd owned Burrell AHO 563 (3807/1919) *Nobby* a compound cylinder tractor recorded at the West Sussex Traction Engine Rally, North Heath, Pulborough on 12 August 1956. *John Meredith/Online Transport Archive (371/7)*

During World War 1 production of traction engines continued although, as with other manufacturing business, Charles Burrell & Sons Ltd was also involved in the production of armaments. With peace, the company became part of the Agricultural & General Engineers combine in 1919; the following year a steam road locomotive was displayed at the Darlington Agricultural Show but, by this date, the tide was turning against steam in favour of the internal combustion engine.

In 1920, the company manufactured the first of the 'scenic' showman's engines; this was No 3827 *Victory* that was supplied to Charles Thurston of Norwich. These 'scenic' engines were built to cope with the increased size of the fairground rides of the period.

Unable to compete with the cheapness of the internal combustion engine, the company closed down on 4 June 1928 with the final products bearing the historic Burrell name actually being produced by Richard Garrett & Sons. The works at Thetford finally closed in 1929; the Agricultural & General Engineers combine was wound up three years later. There is now a museum — the Charles Burrell Museum — in Thetford that opened in 1991 to record the history of a company that was once the biggest employer in the town. The museum is housed in the company's former paint shop on Minstergate.

Edwin Foden, Sons & Co

Based in Sandbach in Cheshire, Foden was one of the best-known manufacturers of steam lorries. Edwin Foden was an apprentice both with Plant & Hancock, a manufacturer of agricultural equipment, and then with the London & North Western Railway. He returned to Plant & Hancock in 1860 at the age of 19 and, when George Hancock retired in 1870, Foden took over having become a partner in Hancock & Foden four years earlier. The business became Edwin Foden and, in 1876, was retitled as

As recorded in *The Engineer* in 1893, this was an 8nhp traction engine supplied by Edwin Foden Sons & Co of Sandbach in Cheshire. *The Engineer*

Edwin Foden & Sons, being incorporated as Edwin Foden, Sons & Co Ltd in 1887. The company's first traction engine was completed in 1881.

Edwin Foden's great innovation was the production of a practical and highly efficient compound steam unit in 1887. This was to prove invaluable in the development of the steam lorry. In 1896, restrictions affecting road transport were relaxed. The new rules permitted the operation of vehicles under three tons to travel

Owned by J Shuttlewood, Foden EU 3764 (13068/1928) *Perseverance* is an overtype tractor and was photographed at the Woburn Park Traction Engine Rally on 5 August 1957. *John Meredith/Online Transport Archive (383/2)*

at up to 12mph without a red flag. As a consequence Foden produced four prototype trucks and, in 1901, supplied a three-ton truck for War Office trials. Generally regarded as a success — despite being placed second in the trial behind a Thornycroft — the lorry was the basis of a number of lorries developed thereafter. In the same year, as a means of raising fresh capital, the company became simply Fodens Ltd.

The bulk of Foden's steam lorries were overtype although a number of, less successful, undertype models were also constructed. In 1902 a five-ton lorry was produced; this continued in production until 1923. Steam propulsion continued to dominate even after the death of Edwin Foden in 1911 and this ultimately led to a major split within the family. Despite the evident success of the internal combustion engine, Fodens Ltd continued to manufacture steam wagons through the 1920s with, for example, the C-type five/six-ton model being launched in 1920. By the end of the decade, however, there was a faction within the controlling family that saw the diesel engine as the future. In 1931 Edwin Richard Foden was forced from the company's board as a result of his advocacy of the diesel engine; aged 62 he went into retirement but his son, Dennis, and a number of other ex-Fodens Ltd employees set up a new company and E R Foden was persuaded to come out of retirement to chair the new company, which became known as ERF Ltd and was also based at Sandbach. The new company produced its first vehicle — diesel engine, of course — in 1933 and was to survive as a manufacturer in Cheshire, despite changed ownership in its later years, until 2002.

This Foden steam tractor (14078/1932) MJ 369 *Mighty Atom* was recorded at Witney in 1954. *J M Jarvis/Online Transport Archive*

Although the decision to adopt diesel engines had led to a split within the Foden family and the creation of ERF, Fodens Ltd was itself to realise that diesel power represented the future and, also in 1931, produced its first diesel lorry — the F1 — and the success of this led to the decision to cease production of steam-powered vehicles. Production of these ceased in 1934; in all a total of 6,500 steam wagons were built. Production of Foden trucks continued through the second half of the 20th century, with a new factory at Sandbach being completed in 1974. However, financial problems led to the company being taken over by Paccar International in 1980. In 1998 Paccar also took over the Leyland Truck plant in Lancashire and all production was concentrated at Leyland. Foden-badged lorries continued to be built at Leyland until July 2006.

John Fowler & Co

Based in Hunslet, Leeds, the company of John Fowler & Co was established by the Wiltshire-born John Fowler. Credited with the invention of the steam-driven ploughing engine, Fowler was born in 1826 to a Quaker corn merchant. At the age of 21 he joined the engineering company of Gilkes Wilson & Co of Middlesbrough. A chance visit to Ireland in 1849, shortly after the potato famine, led him to start to investigate better methods of draining poor land and of ploughing. Initially, the equipment that he designed was horse operated but in 1852 he produced his first steam-powered drainage plough. On 21 October 1852 he received a patent for 'Improvements in Machinery for draining land'.

During the 1850s Fowler produced a number of further improvements to the model and, in 1860, entered into an agreement with Kitson & Hewitson of Hunslet, Leeds for the manufacture of his steam ploughs with Fowler's Steam Plough Works built in Hunslet. The resulting company was initially known as Kitson, Hewitson & Fowler but, from 1863, became John Fowler & Co.

By 1864 the company was employing 400 men and boys but, that year, John Fowler was killed in a hunting accident. The business, however, continued now under the management of Robert Fowler and Robert Eddison and, the following year, produced its first locomotive.

Contemporary illustrations portraying the eight-horse traction engine manufactured by John Fowler & Co in 1869.

Owned at the time by R A Whitehead, Tonbridge, Fowler BP 5767 (9924/1904) is a compound traction engine which, at the time of writing, carries the name *James Penfold*. It is seen at Paddock Wood on 17 August 1957. *John Meredith/Online Transport Archive (386/6)*

By 1871 the company employed 950 and a decade later this had reached 1,100. Throughout this period, the company was continuing to develop and patent improvements to its various types of ploughing equipment. In 1886, the company was incorporated as John Fowler & Co (Leeds) Ltd and by the outbreak of World War 1 was employing almost 3,000 on the manufacture of a wide range of products, including railway engines, traction engines, ploughing engines and road rollers.

After World War 1, the company produced its first steam wagon in 1924; by the time production ceased in 1935 a total of 117 had been built. However, in 1931, the company was to produce its first diesel-powered lorry — the Marathon 6 — and diesel-powered vehicles were increasingly to dominate the company's activities as, with other builders, the production of steam-powered vehicles declined.

In the early 1930s, the company, following advice from Sidney Harrison late of Charles Burrell & Sons, constructed four of the most sophisticated showman's engines built. These B6 'Super Lion' engines were supplied between March 1932 and March 1934 at a time when the use of steam on roads was in terminal decline. Of the four, three — *The Lion* (No 19782 of 1932), *King Carnival II* (No 19783 of 1932) and *Supreme*

Recorded at Knebworth on 2 September 1978, this showman's engine DP 4418 was manufactured by Fowler (14425/1916). At the time of writing the engine carries the name *Carry On*. *J M Jarvis/Online Transport Archive*

Owned at the time by B Dunford, Flockton, Fowler WU 2071 (16485/1925) is a 10-ton steamroller and is seen at Bramham Park on 24 August 1980. *John Meredith/Online Transport Archive (963/9)*

When recorded here at Southwater on 24 June 1956 in the ownership of F R Godden, Fowler YC 3689 (16365/1928) was a compound roller; this engine survives but is now in the guise of a convertible tractor with the name *King of the Road*. *John Meredith/Online Transport Archive (369/6)*

(No 20223 of 1934) — survive into preservation. In 1935, however, the production of steam railway locomotives ceased and, two years later, the company manufactured its last road roller — the final steam-powered road vehicle it produced.

In 1947 the company was taken over by Marshall, Sons & Co Ltd to form Marshall-Fowler Ltd; production at Leeds was concentrated on tractors and diesel railway locomotives. The business in Leeds closed in 1974.

Lancashire Steam Motor Co

James Sumner was the son of a Leyland, Lancashire blacksmith and inherited the business in 1892; wishing to move the business in a different direction, he built a steam lawnmower that achieved success at the Lancashire Agricultural Show. J Sumner Ltd was established in 1895 and, the following year, a share in the business was acquired by Charles Spurrier from Manchester; Spurrier's brother Henry joined Sumner in the business, which was renamed as the Lancashire Steam Motor Co in 1896.

This is a steam wagon built by the Lancashire Steam Motor Co in 1899. This particular model was designed to carry up to four tons.

Initially the business was based at rented property in Herbert Street in Leyland, where around 20 were employed initially in the production of steam lawnmowers. The company's first road vehicle was a steam-powered 1.5-ton van in late 1896; this was followed by the production of a number of undertype steam wagons that used a vertical fire-tube boiler. In 1899 passenger-carrying vehicles were first produced. As the business grew, it relocated to Hough Lane, where 150 were now employed. Whilst the vast majority of the steam vehicles were conventionally fired by coal, the company also produced a number of vehicles that were oil-fired, including a single-deck bus that was supplied to the Dundee & District Tramways Co in 1899.

The basic steam wagon as produced by the Lancashire Steam Motor Co in 1901; this shows to good effect the undertype wagon with vertical boiler that were typical of the company's products. *The Engineer*

The evolution of the Lancashire Steam Motor Co from the original steam van of 1896 (top left) through to the latest product of 1904 (bottom right).

However, the early years of the 20th century saw the business explore the production of petrol-engined vehicles, exhibiting a double-deck bus at the 1905 Commercial Motor Show. Bearing the trademark 'Leyland', the new model proved highly successful and indicated the future direction of the company's production.

In 1907, the company was renamed Leyland Motors Ltd, following the acquisition of Coultard (a Preston-based business that had since 1897 also been manufacturing steam wagons), and a second factory at Chorley was completed. It was to the smaller new factory that production of steam wagons was transferred just before World War 1 when the company relocated its main Leyland site to a new factory at Farrington. By the outbreak of War in 1915 the company had produced some 1,275 petrol-drive wagons as opposed to 415 steam wagons. In 1926 Leyland sold its steam wagon building business to Atkinson Walker Wagons Ltd of Frenchwood Works, Preston. The new owner expanded in 1929 through the acquisition of Mann's Patent Steam Cart & Wagon Co but the combined business was already in difficulties. Steam Wagon production ceased later in 1929 by which date Atkinson had produced 545 steam wagons since production had started in 1916.

Marshall, Sons & Co

In 1842, William Marshall, who had been an agent for William Fairburn & Sons, bought the Back Street Foundry in Gainsborough, Lincolnshire and established a business there six years later for the manufacture of agricultural machinery. In 1849 the factory was renamed the Britannia Ironworks and production started of road steam engines.

An agricultural engine produced by Marshall, Sons & Co in 1876. This was the year that the company produced its first traction engines.

Owned by J O Lugg & Son, this Marshall PL 1564 (85740/1930) is a compound roller and was photographed at Billingshurst on 6 August 1956. *John Meredith/Online Transport Archive (371/4)*

Marshall's two sons — James and Henry — joined the business in 1857 and 1861 respectively and, following the death of William in 1861 the company was incorporated with limited liability. By 1871 the company was employing 606 men and boys and, in 1876, produced its first traction engine. The company continued to grow during the 1870s and, in 1881, employed 1,574 with production now including a wide range of steam engines. By 1914 the company was employing 5,000 and had started, in 1900, the production of tractors with internal-combustion engines. During World War 1 the company manufactured some 150 Bristol F2B fighter aircraft at a new factory established at Lea Road in Gainsborough during 1917.

After the war, the company continued to produce a wide range of equipment, with both steam and internal-combustion vehicles available. In 1925 Marshall, Sons & Co Ltd was contracted by the Greek government to supply 100 of the latest Class S compound steamrollers. Four years later, the company acquired the goodwill of Clayton & Shuttleworth, which had gone into liquidation but, five years later, the economic downturn brought down Marshall as well as the company was forced into receivership.

In October 1935 Thomas W Ward Ltd acquired the business and reorganised it; the workforce by this date, however, had been reduced to 930. Ward's ownership was, however, short-lived as, in March the following year, a new company Marshall, Sons & Co (Successors) Ltd formed which was converted into a public company.

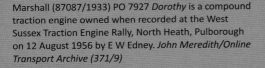

Marshall (87087/1933) PO 7927 *Dorothy* is a compound traction engine owned when recorded at the West Sussex Traction Engine Rally, North Heath, Pulborough on 12 August 1956 by E W Edney. *John Meredith/Online Transport Archive (371/9)*

Originally built for the War Department during World War 1, Ransomes, Sims & Jefferies WT 1271 (26994/1916) is a single cylinder general-purpose engine. It was last used prior to preservation by J T Hymas at Burton Leonard near Harrogate for soil sterilisation and is seen at the Stillinton Rally of 3 August 1968 in the ownership of C J, D R and M R Bartrop of Worksop. *John Meredith/Online Transport Archive (663/4)*

During World War 2 the company continued to manufacture a range of products; these included diesel tractors and rollers, tea machinery and steam plant boilers as well as midget submarines and naval guns. In 1943 the company's name changed to Marshall, Sons & Co Ltd and, in 1947, the company merged with John Fowler & Co Ltd to become Marshall-Fowler Ltd but by this date production of traction engines and other steam-powered vehicles had ceased.

The company continued to be involved in the manufacture of a range of agricultural and other equipment thereafter, becoming part of the Bentall Simplex group. The name 'Marshall' was revived in the 1980s and, in 1982, the rights to the manufacture of the Leyland company's range of tractors was acquired with production being moved to Gainsborough. This was not wholly successful and production ceased in 1992.

The site of the Britannia Ironworks is now occupied by a shopping centre called, appropriately, Marshall's Yard.

Seen in Southport during the spring of 1975, PU 4391 *Old Faithful* is a Ransomes, Sims & Jefferies (35247/1920) compound general-purpose traction engine. *John G Parkinson/Online Transport Archive*

Ransomes, Sims & Jefferies

Based in Ipswich, Ransomes, Sims & Jefferies had interests in a number of engineering products. These ranged from traction engines to combine harvesters and trolleybuses. The origins of the business dated to the late 18th century and Robert Ransome, a native of Norwich who moved to Ipswich in 1789. By accident he discovered the process of chilled casting, for which he received a number of patents. Bringing his sons into the business, the family produced a range of ploughs and other agricultural implements and, from the early 1840s, this was supplemented by the manufacture of steam-powered agricultural equipment such as threshing machines.

The name Ransomes, Sims & Jefferies was registered on 12 May 1884 to take over the business and by the end of the decade the company was offering a wide range of equipment. This included portable, traction, fixed, horizontal and vertical

Ransomes, Sims & Jefferies UD 2296 (39088/1928), owned at the time by G Main, is a 4nhp compound traction engine and was pictured at the Woburn Park Traction Engine Rally on 5 August 1957. Today the vehicle bears the name *Ganymede*. *John Meredith/Online Transport Archive (383/10)*

engines, steam-powered presses and winding engines. At the Royal Agricultural Show held at York in 1900 the company displayed traction and portable engines, threshing machines, horse rakes, ploughing cultivators and lawn mowers. By 1914 the company employed 2,500 with lawn mowers proving to be one of the key products, manufactured in a separate factory established in the town.

After World War 1 much of the company's vehicle production was no longer steam-powered with trolleybuses being produced in numbers and by 1927 the business was controlled by the engine manufacturer Ruston & Hornsby Ltd of Lincoln. In 1956 the steam engine part of Ransomes, Sims & Jefferies was sold to another Lincoln-based manufacturer Robey & Co, although by this date the manufacture of steam-powered vehicles had ceased.

Following the sale Ransomes, Sims & Jefferies continued to produce agricultural equipment and lawn mowers; the former business was sold to Electrolux of Sweden in 1989 and the latter was taken over by Textron Inc of the USA nine years later.

R D Martino's Ransomes, Sims & Jefferies VX 7317 (41046/1930) *Enterprise* is a compound general-purpose traction engine and was recorded at the Saffron Walden Steam Festival on 15 June 1957. *John Meredith/Online Transport Archive (381/9)*

Richard Garrett & Sons

Based at Leiston Works, Leiston, Suffolk, Richard Garrett & Sons was a manufacture of agricultural machinery, steam engines and lorries, trolleybuses and machine tools.

The company's origins were in the late 18th century when Richard Garrett set up as a blacksmith; in 1805 his son, Thomas, took over the business and, the following year, he constructed his first threshing machine. By the 1830s, when Thomas's grandson (also called Thomas), was in charge the production of steam engines commenced. Production extended to portable engines in the 1840s and, by 1861, the business was employing 550 men and boys. Traction engines were initially produced under licence to Aveling but, in 1876, the company produced the first traction engine to its own design. The range of products continued to grow: in 1898, for example, a 10-ton steamroller was built and, six years later, the company produced its first steam lorry.

By the outbreak of World War 1 in 1914 the company's continuing growth had seen the number of employees reach almost 2,000. The range of products included traction engines, road rollers, motor tractors and wagons, and steam threshing

Described as a 'Colonial Compound Road Locomotive', Richard Garrett & Sons Ltd manufactured this traction engine in 1904. At a time when the British Empire was at its peak, exports to the colonies represented a significant proportion of the production from many of the UK's factories.

Below: Built by Garrett BJ 1969 (32048/1914) *Lady Raglan* is a compound 4nhp traction engine. It is seen here at the Witney Rally in August 1954. *J M Jarvis/Online Transport Archive*

equipment. After the war, the company, which became part of Agricultural & General Engineers in 1920, continued to develop steam-powered vehicles, launching the 'Suffolk Punch' (a 40hp steam-powered tractor) in 1925.

The range of products continued to grow during the late 1920s, with trolleybuses being manufactured and the first diesel-engined lorry being completed in 1930. In 1926 the company acquired the Glasgow-based Caledon Motor Co with the result that Caledon vehicles were manufactured at Leiston thereafter. Following the collapse of Agriculture & General Engineers in 1932, Richard Garrett & Sons was acquired by Beyer, Peacock & Co but the factory at Leiston continued under the name of Richard Garrett Engineering Works.

A Garrett CU 4565 (33380/1918) belonging to Langrish Brothers is seen at the West Sussex Traction Engine Rally, North Heath, Pulborough on 12 August 1956. This engine still survives but is now in the form of a showman's engine with extended canopy and has been given the name *Sapphire*. *John Meredith/Online Transport Archive (371/12)*

Manufactured by Garrett in 1929, OU 3239 (35225/1929) is a 4nhp compound traction engine. Seen here at the Lambton Park Rally on 15 June 1958 when it was named *Popeye*, OU 3239 is, at the time of writing, named *Leslie* and has been fitted with a short canopy. *Tony Wickens/Online Transport Archive (2023)*

Vehicle production ceased in the 1930s with the last lorries being completed in 1939. In all the works completed some 22,500 steam engines of which about 20,000 were portable types. Thereafter the site continued to undertake other engineering work until final closure in the late 1970s. Today part of the factory survives as the Long Shop Steam Museum.

Sentinel Waggon Works

The company's origins lay in a business, Alley & MacClellan, that was established in the mid-1870s at Polmadie, Glasgow. In 1906 the company established the Sentinel Waggon Works and produced its first five-ton vertical boiler steam wagon. This featured a two-cylinder undertow engine and chain drive.

In 1915, Alley & McClellan established a new factory at Shrewsbury and transferred the production of steam wagons, along with some staff, to the new site. A new company, Sentinel Waggon Works Ltd, was set up at the same time. Alley & MacClellan continued to operate as an engineering company in Glasgow until the 1950s.

World War 1 was a massive stimulus to the production of road vehicles for use by the military — something that result in significant changes to commercial road haulage after the war — and this was a Sentinel steam wagon supplied to the Royal Navy during the war.

Recorded in 1964, this is a Sentinel-Super tractor 757 CTT (5644/1924) *The Elephant*. Note the picture of the elephant on the vehicle's body behind the crew. *J M Jarvis/Online Transport Archive*

The Sentinel DG4 was introduced in 1926; this example, YD 7509 (8009/1929) was constructed three years later and is seen at the York Historic Commercial Vehicle Rally on 17 September 1989. *John Meredith/Online Transport Archive (1172/8)*

Owned by Thames Tar Products & Contractors Ltd, this Sentinel DG6 (8562/1931) steam lorry — FD 6603 — was photographed at Beddington Lane Depot on 2 December 1950. *John Meredith/Online Transport Archive (158/6)*

Owned by the date of the photograph by J C Butler, Tonbridge, this Sentinel BYL 485 (9208/1935) was S4 wagon and was one of three new to Price's Bakery, Croydon. It is seen at Paddock Wood on 17 August 1957. *John Meredith/Online Transport Archive (385/7)*

Appropriately named *The Shrewsbury Flyer*, this Sentinel S8 steam wagon UJ 3652 (9105/1934) is seen at the Knebworth 'Wonderful World of Wheels' on 2 September 1978. *J M Jarvis/Online Transport Archive*

The new company hit financial problems and was reorganised as Sentinel Waggon Works (1920) Ltd shortly after the end of World War 1 with ownership now completely separated from the original Scottish company. Production of the Super Sentinel was introduced in 1923; using a production line model similar to that pioneered by Henry Ford, the company was able to manufacture 1,500 of the new model. In all some 4,500 of the original Sentinel had been built by 1923 since its introduction in 1906.

Apart from the production of steam wagons, a business that Sentinel and Foden dominated, from the 1920s, Sentinel also manufactured railway locomotives — steam initially but later diesel (the last steam locomotives were built in 1958, the following year saw the first diesel engines tested) — along with railcars, many of the latter in co-operation with Cammell, Laird & Co.

During the 1920s and 1930s, Sentinel produced a range of steam wagons. Following the Super Sentinel came the DG4, which was launched in 1926, the DG6, the DG8 (1929), the S4 (1934), the S6 and the S8. The S-type featured a single-acting four-cylinder underfloor engine. In all, 3,750 steam wagons were produced between 1935 and 1952, when the manufacture of steam wagons ceased.

In 1936 the company went public as Sentinel Waggon Works (1936) Ltd becoming Sentinel (Shrewsbury) Ltd in 1947; reflecting the decline in the steam wagon business — legislation in the 1930s had made the production of steam wagons more difficult as the law required lighter lorries — the new company produced its first diesel-powered road vehicle shortly after the end of World War 2 and, in 1948, launched its first bus design at the Commercial Motor Show.

Engineering continued at the Sentinel Works after the end of steam wagon production (the last order, in 1949, was for 100 to be supplied to Argentina); ownership of the site eventually passed to Rolls-Royce, who purchased the business in 1956 (when diesel lorry production ceased). Much of the factory complex is still extant and engineering continues, although ownership has changed hands on several occasions since 1956.

Wallis & Steevens

The Basingstoke-based company of Wallis & Steevens was originally established in 1856 by Arthur Wallis and Charles Haslam as Wallis & Haslam. Occupying the North Hants Ironworks, the company was joined by Charles Steevens in 1861. The company initially produced threshing machines and other agricultural equipment and became Wallis & Steevens on the retirement of Haslam in 1869.

This Wallis & Stevens-built traction engine was demonstrated at the Royal Agricultural Show in 1895, which was held near Darlington.

A Wallis & Stevens single roller HO 6417 (7247/1912) belonging to F R Godden recorded at Southwater on 24 June 1956. *John Meredith/Online Transport Archive (369/5)*

D Kilburn's Wallis & Steevens HO 2779 (7637/1918) — a compound tractor — is pictured at the West Sussex Traction Engine Rally, North Heath, Pulborough on 12 August 1956. *John Meredith/Online Transport Archive (371/6)*

Dr C J Romane's Wallis & Stevens agricultural engine BL 795 (7683/1919) *Eileen* is seen at the National Traction Engine Rally at Appleford on 6 June 1953. *John Meredith/Online Transport Archive (303/11)*

Although drawings for possible steam engines date to the 1860s, it was not until 1877 that the company produced its first traction engine. This was named *Success* and over the next few years the company did achieve some considerable success in the manufacture of steam engines and its range of products grew. In 1890 the company produced its first steamroller and, in 1895 two years before the business became public, it produced its first road locomotive. In 1906 the company produced its first steam wagon and production of this type of vehicle was to continue through to 1925.

In 1923 the company launched the first of its 'Advance' series of steamrollers; this heralded a period when the company increasingly came to produce rollers alone. These were initially steam but later petrol- and diesel-powered versions came to dominate and manufacture of steamrollers ceased during the 1930s.

Production of road rollers continued at the original site until 1966 when redevelopment of the site resulted in a move to a new factory; production continued there until 1981 when the business was wound-up. Agreement was reached for BSP International Foundations Ltd of Ipswich to take over all of Wallis & Steevens' designs and production, with the transfer being completed in July 1981.

Above: Built by Wallis & Steevens in 1928, OT 8512 (7940/1928) *Susie* is a road roller captured in the colours of N A C Melhuish of Chipping Norton at the Witney Rally in August 1954. *J M Jarvis/Online Transport Archive*

Right: A Wallis & Steevens Ltd steam roller OU 2684 (8005/1929) *Advance* belonging to H Woodham & Sons Ltd is recorded on Westminster Bridge Road, London on 9 November 1950. *John Meredith/Online Transport Archive (155/12)*

Described as a new road locomotive, this traction engine was one constructed by William Foster & Co Ltd in 1903.

William Foster & Co Ltd

The Lincoln-based company of William Foster & Co had its origins in 1846 when William Foster acquired a flour mill in the city and started the manufacture of agricultural machinery. A decade later, in 1856, the mill became a foundry — Wellington Foundry — where, in 1858, Foster produced his first portable steam engine.

By 1861 Foster was employing 80 men in total, a number that had increased to 129 a decade later. In 1877 the company was incorporated as William Foster & Co Ltd and in 1889 built its first self-propelled traction engine. In 1899 the company moved to a new site, located between Wellington Street and Firth Road in Lincoln, where a new factory — again called Wellington Foundry — was established.

During World War 1 the company built the first tanks used by the British army; after the war, the Royal Commission on Awards to Inventors concluded that the joint inventors of the tanks were Major W G Wilson and Sir William Tritton, the managing director of William Foster & Co Ltd.

After the war was over, the company's range of steam-powered vehicles increased. In 1919 it launched a steam roller; between then and 1933 when production ceased, a total of 60 were built. In 1920, at the Darlington Royal Agricultural Show, the company exhibited steam wagons fitted with compound engines. Production of traction engines continued until 1942, when the company produced the final traction engine to be built commercially in Britain.

In 1927 the company had a working arrangement with Gwynnes Ltd (then in liquidation), a manufacturer of centrifugal pumps, based in Hammersmith to acquire the business and the foundry in west London. Production was, however, moved to Lincoln in 1930, where manufacture of pumps ceased in 1968.

William Foster & Co Ltd's independent existence ended in 1960 when the business was acquired by W H Allen, Sons & Co. The Wellington Foundry closed with the end of pump production; although used briefly by Ruston Bucyrus in the early 1970s, the site had been subsequently cleared and is now occupied by a retail park.

This Foster CT 3896 (3682/1908) — a 6nhp single traction — was new to Daniel Stanton of Baston, Lincolnshire and used for threshing until 1955. It is seen here at the Woburn Park Traction Engine Rally on 5 August 1957 when owned by D F Knight. *John Meredith/Online Transport Archive (384/5)*

New to the High Wycombe Chair Co, when recorded at the Woburn Park Traction Engine Rally on 5 August 1957 this Foster 4nhp compound tractor PP 7306 (14378/1925) was in the ownership of H D Knight. *John Meredith/Online Transport Archive (383/11)*

This 4nhp compound traction engine PN 5629 (now named *Ikanopit*) was built by Foster in 1930 (14608/1930) and is seen here at the Witney Rally of August 1954. *J M Jarvis/Online Transport Archive*

Preservation

By the late 1950s, use of traction engines — with the exception of steamrollers — had virtually ceased. The process of replacing steam with petrol- and diesel-fuelled vehicles accelerated after the end of World War 2 when, as in 1919, a significant number of military surplus vehicles came onto the market. The last use of a showman's engine in commercial use was in 1958 before the engine was sold for scrap.

This was, however, not to be the end of the story as the preservation movement had already started. In 1954, for example, the National Traction Engine Trust was established in the UK; this is now an umbrella organisation with some 30 other clubs worldwide affiliated to it. These include the Road Locomotive Society and the Road Roller Association. A significant number of British-built traction engines and other steam road vehicles have survived into preservation. Looking at the major manufacturers, some 329 vehicles produced by Charles Burrell & Sons are believed to survive along with121 from Richard Garrett & Sons, 117 from Foden, 117 from Sentinel and 444 from Marshall, Sons & Co. As with other types of preservation, these vehicles are to be found in a variety of conditions, from near scrap to pristine, and some vehicles that were still extant in the 1950s are possibly no longer in existence. Many of the vehicles illustrated in this book at rallies in the 1950s are known still to be around although may not have been seen for some years.

The profile of traction engine preservation was raised in recent years through the activities of the late Fred Dibnah, who originally bought a 1910 Aveling & Porter steamroller for £175. After restoration, the steamroller was used by Dibnah to travel to steam fairs around the country. He subsequently purchased a 1912 Aveling & Porter traction engine (TA 2436; 7838/1912) in 1980 for £2,300; restored eventually, the vehicle was used in Dibnah's final television work. Following his death in 2004, the convertible general-purpose engine was used to pull a trailer with his coffin and trademark cloth cap. It was subsequently sold for £240,000. The value of this traction engine demonstrates how much the cost of preservation has increased since the late 1950s when engines could be acquired for less than £100.

One of the more unfortunate trends in traction engine preservation is the conversion, in preservation, of a number of other models into showman's engines as the latter command a higher price and are perceived as being more prestigious. This has particularly affected less glamorous types, in particular road rollers.

Above: The line-up of preserved engines is one of the great features of traction engine rallies; this impressive collection was recorded at the Witney Rally held in August 1954. *J M Jarvis/Online Transport Archive*

Right: When recorded in preservation at Gaddesdon Row in August 1966, HO 5834 was a Wallis & Steevens (2656/1903) was a steamroller. Since that date, the vehicle has been converted into a single-cylinder tractor with short canopy and with its rollers replaced by wheels. Today, it bears the name *Little Olga*. *J M Jarvis/Online Transport Archive*

Index